Courting Justice

Landmark Supreme Court Case Can Offer Justice for U.S. Victims of Iranian Terror

Foundation for Defense of
Democracies
Introduction by Mark Dubowitz

INTRODUCTION TO SUPREME COURT *AMICUS CURIAE* BRIEF IN SUPPORT OF RESPONDENTS IN THE CASE OF BANK MARKAZI V. PETERSON

By Mark Dubowitz
Executive Director, Foundation for Defense of
Democracies

In the summer of 2015, the United States and its international partners agreed to a fatally flawed agreement with the Islamic Republic of Iran over its nuclear program. The deal provides the Iranian regime with billions of dollars in sanctions relief for term-limited constraints on certain nuclear activities. At the same time, the agreement does not expunge Iran's decades-long rap-sheet of terrorist activities, including terrorist attacks against American service members and citizens.

Since the deal was announced, Iranian aggression has not subsided, in fact quite the opposite. Iran, regarded by the U.S. Department of State as the leading state sponsor of terrorism, continues to engage in violent and illicit activities including aggressive behavior towards its neighbors. Iran remains unrepentant about its history of global terrorism and continues to defy international norms through its support of terrorist proxies throughout the Middle East and Bashar al-Assad's regime in Syria, its systemic illicit finance and money laundering activities, and its gross human rights abuses.

In this context, on January 13, 2016, the U.S. Supreme Court heard oral arguments in a critical case affecting America's ability to use economic tools to advance its national interest. In *Bank Markazi v. Peterson*, the

Supreme Court will determine whether American victims of Iranian terrorism will be able to collect on judgments won against Iran from funds belonging to the Central Bank of Iran, which are being held in a New York bank. To date, Iran has refused to pay judgments rendered against it and has defied court decisions ordering compensation for victims of terrorism.

The district court and the court of appeals have previously ruled in favor of the American victims. The Central Bank of Iran, also known as Bank Markazi, has appealed, challenging the constitutionality of the Iran Threat Reduction and Syrian Human Rights Act of 2012 (ITRA), which removed sovereign immunity protections from the assets in question and clarified that these assets could be used to settle outstanding claims against Iran. Congress included a specific provision in the law in order to make it easier for victims of terrorism to receive compensation.

The legislation, which was the result of nearly two decades of congressional efforts to address Iranian support for terrorism, nuclear proliferation, and regional aggression, was supported by overwhelming bipartisan majorities of both houses of Congress and was signed into law by President Barack Obama. The legislation targeted key sectors of the Iranian economy including energy, shipping, banking, and insurance in order to reduce the amount of oil and other commercial revenues the Iranian regime could devote to advancing its illicit nuclear and ballistic missile programs, supporting terrorism, and repressing its citizens.

The Foundation for Defense of Democracies (FDD), a non-partisan, Washington, DC-based think tank, filed an *amicus curiae* (friend of the court) brief arguing that ITRA is "a critical tool in the United States' sustained efforts to use economic sanctions to punish Iran for, and deter it from, supporting acts of terrorism against U.S. citizens." The law was intended specifically to ensure not only that the victims of Iranian terrorism are compensated for their suffering but also that *Iran itself* is held accountable for its deplorable acts of state-sponsored terrorism. The brief emerged as part of FDD's work on Iran and terrorism that has spanned more than a decade. Through its Iran Project and its Center on Sanctions and Illicit Finance (CSIF), FDD conducts extensive research on ways to use sanctions to target the economic and financial resources of the Iranian regime as a means of holding it accountable for its illicit activities.

The Supreme Court's decision in the pending case may have implications beyond the legal issues under consideration. The Iranian regime is attempting to use the American legal system to undercut the U.S. government's ability to use economic tools to advance U.S. national security. This case is about more than whether a specific provision of ITRA violates the separation of powers principle; it is about America's ability to use all of the tools of statecraft to push back against Iran's rogue actions.

Coinciding with the implementation of the Iran nuclear agreement, the case serves as an important reminder that Iran's illicit activities extend well-beyond the nuclear realm. Economic tools play a central role in the execution of American foreign policy, and the U.S. government must use all the instruments of statecraft in its efforts to combat threats to America's national security.

No. 14-770

In the

Supreme Court of the United States

BANK MARKAZI, THE CENTRAL BANK OF IRAN

Petitioner,

v.

DEBORAH D. PETERSON, ET AL.,

Respondents.

On Writ of Certiorari to the United States Court of Appeals for the Second Circuit

---

BRIEF FOR *AMICUS CURIAE* FOUNDATION FOR DEFENSE OF DEMOCRACIES IN SUPPORT OF RESPONDENTS

ERIN E. MURPHY
 Counsel of Record
MICHAEL D. LIEBERMAN
Bancroft PLLC
500 New Jersey Avenue, NW
Seventh Floor
Washington, DC 20001
(202) 234-0090
emurphy@bancroftpllc.com

Counsel for Amicus Curiae

12/23/15

1

Table of Contents

TABLE OF AUTHORITIES

Cases

3

STATEMENT OF INTEREST[1]

The Foundation for Defense of Democracies ("FDD") is a non-profit, non-partisan section 501(c)(3) policy institute focusing on foreign policy and national security. Through its Iran Project and its Center on Sanctions and Illicit Finance, FDD conducts extensive research on ways to use sanctions to target the economic and financial resources of the Iranian regime. FDD's work has informed numerous pieces of Iran sanctions legislation, including the Iran Freedom and Counter-Proliferation Act of 2012; the Iran Threat Reduction and Syria Human Rights Act of 2012; section 1245 of the National Defense Authorization Act of 2012; and the Comprehensive Iran Sanctions, Accountability, and Divestment Act of 2010. These laws target Iran's energy, financial, shipping, insurance, commercial, and proliferation activities, as well as the regime's human rights abuses. The legislative measures are widely viewed as the most robust U.S. measures yet imposed against the Iranian regime.

FDD also seeks to reduce the amount of oil and other commercial revenues the Iranian regime can devote to advancing its illicit nuclear and ballistic missile programs, supporting terrorism, and repressing its citizens. As part of this effort, FDD has performed studies on sanctioning Iran's Central Bank, Iranian banks, and the Islamic Revolutionary Guard Corps, and has sought to deny the Islamic Republic the ability to use the international Society for Worldwide Interbank Financial Telecommunications ("SWIFT") to conduct financial transactions.

---

[1] Pursuant to Supreme Court Rule 37.6, *amicus curiae* states that no counsel for any party authored this brief in whole or in part and that no entity or person, aside from *amicus curiae*, its members, and its counsel, made any monetary contribution toward the preparation or submission of this brief. Pursuant to Supreme Court Rule 37.3, counsel of record for all parties have consented to this filing in letters on file with the Clerk's office.

FDD has a significant interest in this case because it provided research, analysis, and expertise to Congress regarding the Iran Threat Reduction and Syria Human Rights Act of 2012, section 502 of which (codified at 22 U.S.C. §8772) is being challenged in this case. In particular, FDD provided extensive research and championed measures in the Act dealing with energy, shipping, banking, insurance, nonproliferation, and human rights abuses. FDD firmly believes that Congress and the President must remain unfettered in their efforts to hold Iran accountable for sponsoring acts of terrorism against U.S. citizens around the world, and that Iran should not be permitted to use the international banking system to shield its assets from terrorism-related judgments. Section 502 of the Act is instrumental to those efforts.

SUMMARY OF ARGUMENT

This case is not about "a statute that effectively directs a particular result in a single pending case." Pet'r.Br.i. Nor is it about an effort by Congress "to ensure that its favored litigant prevails." *Id.* at 2. Instead, it is about a statute that serves as a critical tool in the United States' sustained efforts to use economic sanctions to punish Iran for, and deter it from, supporting acts of terrorism against U.S. citizens. Consistent with that broader foreign policy objective, the statute is not confined to any particular litigant or to any particular claim. Nor does the statute direct a federal court to order one party to turn over money to another. Instead, the statute just establishes the law that a court should apply when determining whether a particular set of assets is subject to execution and attachment for judgments against Iran, and then tasks a court with applying it. The findings that the statute tasks the court with making are no mere make-weights; nor are they fig leafs for congressional incursion on Article III prerogative. Instead, they are precisely what ensures that execution or attachment will be permitted only when it will further both of the policy goals underlying the law: facilitating efforts by the victims of Iran's deplorable actions to collect on the judgments they have obtained, and ensuring that Iran itself is held responsible for the injuries it has caused.

Petitioner's blithe suggestion that "[i]f Congress wanted to compensate these plaintiffs," it could have just paid their claims itself, Pet'r.Br.53, ignores what section 8772 is really about. To be sure, section 8772 is intended to ensure that the representatives of the hundreds of the victims who lost their lives to Iran's state-sponsored terrorism will actually be compensated for the wrongs that they have suffered. But equally important, it is also about achieving the United States' broader foreign policy objective of using economic sanctions to ensure that *Iran itself* is held responsible for the deplorable acts of terrorism that it sponsors, and meaningfully deterred from continuing to do the same. And the statute is carefully crafted to leave fully intact a court's Article III prerogative to determine whether the legal conditions Congress has crafted to further those twin policy goals are actually satisfied. The statute thus simply does not implicate any of the separation of powers principles on which petitioner seeks to rely. In short, it is Iran, not section 8772, that is a threat to our democracy.

ARGUMENT

.I   **Section 8772 Is Part Of A Comprehensive Effort To Use Economic Sanctions To Punish And Deter Iran's Sponsorship Of Terrorism.**

Section 8772 and the comprehensive 56-page piece of legislation through which it was enacted are part of a sustained effort to use targeted economic sanctions to punish and deter Iran's sponsorship of terrorism. Since the Iran Hostage Crisis in 1979, Iran has posed a continuous and uninterrupted threat to American interests and American lives. Iran-sponsored bombings, assassinations, hijackings, and hostage-takings over the past 36 years have claimed thousands of victims, and future acts threaten to claim thousands more. This pervasive Iranian threat is virtually without parallel in the modern era, in terms of both its longevity and its intensity. American foreign

8

policymakers have accordingly used every means of national power and leverage at their disposal to ensure that Iran is held accountable for, and deterred from, harming U.S. citizens.

From the beginning, economic sanctions have been a critical tool in the United States' foreign policy toward Iran. *See* Kenneth Katzman, Cong. Research Serv., RS 20871, *Iran Sanctions* 1 (2015) ("Katzman"). During the Iran Hostage Crisis, President Carter declared a national emergency and blocked billions of dollars of Iranian assets held in the United States. *See Dames & Moore v. Regan*, 453 U.S. 654, 662-63 (1981). Although most of those sanctions were lifted upon resolution of the crisis in 1981, the United States officially designated Iran a state sponsor of terrorism following the October 1983 bombing of United States Marine barracks in Lebanon. That designation triggered substantial sanctions under the Export Administration Act of 1979, including restrictions on foreign assistance, a ban on arms transfers, and export controls for dual-use items. *See* Katzman 2-3.

In the mid-1990s, President Clinton and Congress continued efforts to deny Iran financial resources to support terrorism. President Clinton issued several executive orders with respect to Iran, including bans on United States investment in Iran's energy sector and bans on United States trade with Iran. *See* Exec. Order No. 12,957, 60 Fed. Reg. 14,615 (1995); Exec. Order No. 12,959, 60 Fed. Reg. 24,757 (1995). In 1996, Congress went one step further with the Iran and Libya Sanctions Act ("ILSA"), Pub. L. No. 104-172, 110 Stat. 1541 (1996), which sought to deprive Iran of foreign investment in its energy sector. The ILSA mandated sanctions on foreign entities or persons investing more than $20 million in Iran's energy sector. *See* Katzman 8-11.

Beginning in 2006, the Bush administration and then the Obama administration, with bipartisan support from Congress, designed a new and unprecedented campaign of economic pressure on Iran. These efforts began with the Department of the Treasury, which worked to persuade banks around the world to cease all business with Iran and isolate Iran from the international financial system. To ensure that Iran could not get around those constraints by funneling its assets through third parties, President Bush issued two executive orders that blocked the assets of individual Iranian banks and other entities that Iran has used to facilitate its sponsorship of terrorism. *See* Exec. Order No. 13,224, 66 Fed. Reg. 49,079 (2001); Exec. Order No. 13,382, 70 Fed. Reg. 38,567 (2005). The State Department also engaged with the United Nations Security Council, which passed four sanctions resolutions against Iran between 2006 and 2010. Katzman 31-32. These resolutions froze the assets of named Iranian individuals and entities, prohibited Iran from a wide range of weapons-related activity, prohibited certain exports to Iran, and called for restraints on transactions with Iranian banks. *Id.* at 32.

Congress has supported these efforts with legislation increasing the economic pressure to deter and prevent Iran from sponsoring terrorism. Between 2010 and 2013, congressional sanctions targeted Iran's financial, energy, shipping, automotive, petrochemical, insurance, precious metals, and industrial trade industries. These efforts cut off Iran's economic and financial lifelines, including its crude oil exports, the Central Bank of Iran's access to the global financial system, and the use of the SWIFT global financial messaging system. First, in 2010, Congress codified the ban on United States trade with Iran in the Comprehensive Iran Sanctions, Accountability, and Divestment Act ("CISADA"), Pub. L. No. 111-195, 124 Stat. 1312 (2010). CISADA also directs the President to impose sanctions on persons who invest in Iran's energy sector, on foreign banks that knowingly facilitate certain Iranian transactions, and on individuals complicit in human rights abuses. In 2011, Congress passed legislation aimed at weakening Iran's oil industry by imposing consequences on foreign banks that process any payments through Iran's central bank. *See* National Defense Authorization Act ("NDAA"), Pub. L. No. 112-81, 125 Stat. 1298 (2011).

The Iran Threat Reduction and Syria Human Rights Act of 2012, Pub. L. No. 112-158, 126 Stat. 1214, is a continuation of these legislative efforts. The Act aims to compel Iran to abandon its pursuit of nuclear weapons, to deter Iran from sponsoring acts of terror, and to punish Iran for its past sponsorship of terrorism. Various provisions of the Act blacklist Iran's energy, financial, and transportation sectors, cut off companies that do business with Iran from access to domestic markets, impose sanctions to prevent Iran from repatriating any proceeds from its oil sales, and deprive the Iranian regime of 80 percent of its hard currency earnings and half the funds that support its budget. Section 8772, the provision at issue in this case, is but one of the Act's many efforts to increase the financial pressure on Iran to cease sponsoring acts of terrorism. "[I]n furtherance of the broader goals of th[e] Act to sanction Iran," section 8772 ensures that Iran will not be able to escape the financial consequences of its actions, or the deterrence that those consequences are intended to accomplish, by using third parties to conceal and/or shield its assets from the many victims of terrorism whose duly obtained judgments Iran has refused to pay.

To that end, section 8772 identifies nearly $2 billion in Iranian assets held at a U.S. bank and subjects those assets to execution to satisfy judgments arising out of Iran's sponsorship of terrorism so long as certain statutorily specified criteria are satisfied. In particular, because section 8772 is intended not just to compensate victims, but also "to ensure that *Iran* is held accountable for paying the judgments" that result from its support of terrorism, the provision applies only if the court determines that "Iran holds equitable title to, or the beneficial interest in, the assets … and that no other person possesses a constitutionally protected interest in the assets." 22 U.S.C. §8772(a)(2) (emphasis added). If the court finds that someone else holds a "beneficial" or "a constitutionally protected interest in the assets," it may make the assets available for execution or attachment only to the extent that doing so "does not infringe upon" that third-party interest. *Id.* §8772(a)(2)(B).

While the statute identifies the relevant assets by reference to the docket number of ongoing proceedings in the Southern District of New York, it does not single out any particular judgment or judgments that they may be used to satisfy. Instead, so long as the conditions that the statute identifies are satisfied, the assets may be used "to satisfy *any* judgment to the extent of any compensatory damages awarded against Iran for damages for personal injury or death caused by an act of torture, extrajudicial killing, aircraft sabotage, or hostage-taking, or the provision of material support or resources for such an act." *Id.* §8772(a)(1)(C) (emphasis added). Accordingly, although section 8772 applies only to one particular proceeding, its application is not confined to the parties who were already part of that proceeding when the statute was enacted. Section 8772 instead leaves other victims of Iran's sponsorship of terrorism free to intervene in the proceeding and assert their own claims to the assets, which some did after the statute took effect. *See* Pet.App.18a-19a.

The provisions of section 8772 thus work in tandem to achieve Congress' two basic objectives. First, in furtherance of its goal of holding Iran responsible for the acts of terrorism that it has sponsored, the statute renders the assets subject to attachment only to the extent that they are, in fact, Iran's assets. Second, in further of its goal of ensuring that *all* victims of Iran's acts have the potential to execute on the judgments they have obtained, the Act renders the assets subject to execution or attachment by *any* victim with a claim against the assets, not just some preferred individual or individuals. The statute requires only that everyone falling into that class litigate their claims in a single consolidated proceeding.

.II Section 8772 Implicates None Of The Separation Of Powers Concerns On Which Petitioner Relies.

When section 8772 is viewed against that backdrop, three things are crystal clear. First, the statute is not directed at "a single pending case." Pet'r.Br.1. It is instead directed at an entire class of cases that Congress just decided to effectively consolidate into a single proceeding. Second, section 8772 does not direct the district court to reach any particular outcome; it instead requires the court to make findings essential to ensuring that the statute furthers not only Congress' interest in compensating the victims of acts of terrorism sponsored by Iran, but also its equally important objective of holding *Iran* responsible for its deplorable actions. Third, section 8772 is nothing like the kinds of one-off laws to which petitioner analogizes. It reflects not congressional interference in a private dispute, but rather a critical component of a much broader foreign policy initiative.

1. First, the notion that section 8772 applies only to "a single pending case" blinks reality. Respondents are the representatives of hundreds of Americans killed in several different Iran-sponsored terrorist attacks, who among them hold judgments from well over a dozen different civil actions.[2] The terrorist attacks giving rise to these judgments include the 1983 Beirut Marine Barracks Bombing, the 1983 kidnapping of CNN

---

[2]   Those civil actions are: *Peterson v. Islamic Republic of Iran*, Nos. 01-cv-2094 and 01-cv-2684 (D.D.C.); *Greenbaum v. Islamic Republic of Iran*, No. 02-cv-2148 (D.D.C.); *Acosta v. Islamic Republic of Iran*, No. 06-cv-745 (D.D.C.); *Rubin v. Islamic Republic of Iran*, No. 01-cv-1655 (D.D.C.); *Estate of Heiser v. Islamic Republic of Iran*, Nos. 00-cv-2329 and 01-cv-2104 (D.D.C); *Levin v. Islamic Republic of Iran*, No. 05-cv-2494 (D.D.C.); *Valore v. Islamic Republic of Iran*, No. 03-cv-1959 (D.D.C); *Bonk v. Islamic Republic of Iran*, No. 08-cv-1273 (D.D.C); *Estate of Silvia v. Islamic Republic of Iran*, No. 06-cv-750 (D.D.C.); *Estate of Brown v. Islamic Republic of Iran*, No. 08-cv-531 (D.D.C); *Estate of Bland v. Islamic Republic of Iran*, No. 05-cv-2124 (D.D.C); *Beer v. Islamic Republic of Iran*, Nos. 06-cv-473 and 08-cv-1807 (D.D.C); *Kirschenbaum. v. Islamic Republic of Iran*, Nos. 03-cv-1708 and 08-cv-1814 (D.D.C); *Arnold v. Islamic Republic of Iran*, No. 06-cv-516 (D.D.C.); *Murphy v. Islamic Republic of Iran*, No. 06-cv-596 (D.D.C.); and *Wultz v. Islamic Republic of Iran*, No. 08-cv-1460 (D.D.C.). Three other plaintiff groups previously were involved in these proceedings, but the district court denied them turnover because they did not yet hold judgments against Iran. *See* Pet.App.19a-20a, 28a. Those civil actions are: *Mwila v. Islamic Republic of Iran*, No. 08-cv-1377 (D.D.C.); *Owens v. Republic of Sudan*, No. 01-cv-2244 (D.D.C.); and *Khaliq v. Republic of Sudan*, No. 10-cv-356 (D.D.C.).

correspondent Jerry Levin, the 1990 assassination of Rabbi Meir Kahane, the 1996 bombing of the Khobar Towers in Saudi Arabia, a September 4, 1997 suicide bombing at a street mall in Jerusalem, an August 9, 2001 suicide bombing at a restaurant in Jerusalem, a December 1, 2001 suicide bombing at a street mall in Jerusalem, a June 11, 2003 suicide bombing on a bus in Jerusalem, and an April 17, 2006 suicide bombing at a restaurant in Tel Aviv.

To be sure, the plaintiffs who obtained judgments in those different cases are now all part of a single proceeding to collect on them. But that is not because their discrete cases are all really one and the same. It is because section 8772 effectively directed everyone who falls into the class of cases to which the law applies—namely, cases in which a victim of Iran's state-sponsored terrorism has obtained a judgment on which he or she is seeking to collect—to go litigate their efforts to execute on the relevant assets in that consolidated proceeding. By declaring section 8772 inapplicable to "any proceedings other than proceedings referred to in subsection (b)," Congress thus did not "change[] the law for a single case." Pet'r.Br.40. Instead, it simply established a single procedural vehicle through which all of the cases to which section 8772 applies could be resolved at once.

That alone cannot be the difference between a constitutional law and an unconstitutional one. If it were, then section 8772 would have been perfectly permissible if Congress had just omitted the language rendering the law inapplicable to "any proceedings other than proceedings referred to in subsection (b)"—even though doing so would have left the law with the exact same substantive effect on the exact same range of cases. Congress does not work any fundamental incursion on Article III prerogative by instructing a single court to resolve a common set of claims brought by several different parties rather than requiring several different courts to do so one by one.

Accordingly, whatever the Constitution may have to say about laws that target "a single pending case," Pet'r.Br.1, there is no need for this Court to resolve that question here, as the answer simply does not have any bearing on this case. Section 8772 does not change the law for a particular *case*; it changes the law for a particular *set of assets*. Any concerns that kind of targeted legislation may raise have no more to do with separation of powers principles than changing the law for a particular bridge, *Pennsylvania v. Wheeling & Belmont Bridge Co.*, 59 U.S. (18 How.) 421 (1855), or for 13 particular forests, *Robertson v. Seattle Audubon Soc'y*, 503 U.S. 429 (1992). *See infra* Part III.B. That does not change just because Congress has coupled a narrow substantive law with a narrow procedural mechanism for invoking it. The Constitution simply does not prevent Congress from trying to ease the burden on victims of acts of terrorism that occurred more than a decade ago (if not longer) by giving them a single forum in which one court can resolve common issues arising out of their efforts to finally collect on the many judgments that their different cases have produced.

2. Second, section 8772 does not dictate—whether "effectively" or otherwise—the outcome of the cases that it governs. The conditions section 8772 imposes on execution of the assets in question in the subsection entitled "Court determination required" are not make-weights designed to cover up an effort to deprive the judiciary of its Article III power. They are critical components of the substantive law that section 8772 creates, included to ensure that the statute will allow execution or attachment only if doing so furthers *both* of the interests Congress sought to achieve.

Again, Congress was not simply looking to transfer wealth to a favored party, or even just to ensure that victims of the acts of terrorism that Iran has sponsored have a remedy for the wrongs they have suffered. Congress also wanted section 8772 to serve the equally important interest of holding *Iran itself* responsible for its role in those deplorable acts. As the government has explained time and again, one of the core goals of economic sanctions is to use financial pressure not just to punish Iran for its past acts, but to get Iran to cease sponsoring acts of terrorism in the future. Accordingly, when Congress required the court to find that the assets in question belong to Iran, and Iran alone, it was not reverse-engineering a legal test that would ensure that the court reached its preferred outcome. It was instead crafting a legal standard that maps directly onto the foreign policy concerns that section 8772 seeks to achieve.

To be sure, Congress may have had very good reason to believe that "Iran holds equitable title to, or the beneficial interest in, the assets" in question, "and that no other person possesses a constitutionally protected interest in th[ose] assets." 22 U.S.C. §8772(a)(2). But whether Congress *expected* the court to reach certain answers to those questions does not change the fact that it did not *instruct* the court to do so. Indeed, the statute expressly contemplates the possibility that the district court could have found that Iran was *not* the only party with a "beneficial interest" in the assets, and creates a distinct rule to govern if the court were to make such a determination. *See id.* Congress can hardly be accused of "effectively dictating" the outcome of the proceeding when its own statute expressly recognizes that the district court could have reached a different result. Petitioner's decision not to dispute section 8772's requirements does not reflect that those requirements were meaningless; at most, it simply suggests that petitioner realized that disputing them would reveal the flaws in its separation of powers arguments.

Moreover, Congress did not confine section 8772 to any particular judgment or persons. It instead again set forth a standard by which the court is to determine whether the law applies, requiring the court to make an independent assessment of whether a claimant is, in fact, seeking to collect on a judgment for "compensatory damages awarded against Iran for damages for personal injury or death caused by an act of torture, extrajudicial killing, aircraft sabotage, or hostage-taking, or the provision of material support or resources for such an act." 22 U.S.C. §8772(a)(1)(C). Sure enough, the district court denied turnover to three of the groups of plaintiffs that were part of this consolidated action when section 8772 was enacted because it found that those plaintiffs did not hold qualifying judgments. *See* Pet.App.19a-20a, 28a. At any rate, again, that Congress may have anticipated which claimants would satisfy that standard is beside the point. What matters for constitutional purposes is that the statute leaves it in the court's hands, not Congress', to determine whether an individual who invokes the law falls within its reach.

Accordingly, any constitutional constraints on Congress' power to "effectively dictate" the outcome of litigation are, once again, not implicated here. Section 8772 does not compel the district court to reach any particular conclusion at all, let alone compel the court to do so in a manner that intrudes on Article III prerogative. *See infra* Part III.A. It simply establishes the criteria that must be satisfied in order for the relevant assets to be subject to execution, and then directs the court to make its own determination of whether that criteria is satisfied.

3. Finally, section 8772 bears no resemblance to the kinds of one-off statutes to which petitioner analogizes. Starting with petitioner's "most salient example," Pet'r.Br.34, the Terri Schiavo legislation was a one-off statute unrelated to any broader legislative effort. When Congress created federal court jurisdiction to hear claims on Terri Schiavo's behalf, Congress was not in the midst of some decades-long initiative to strike a proper balance between state and federal court jurisdiction in family disputes about medical treatment. Congress entered the fray for one case, and one case only. Indeed, whereas the Iran Threat Reduction and Syria Human Rights Act is 56 pages long and contains a wide range of provisions "in furtherance of [Congress'] broader goals ... to sanction Iran," 22 U.S.C. §8772(a)(2), the Act for the Relief of the Parents of Theresa Marie Schiavo was two pages long and did nothing other than create federal court jurisdiction for a single case. *See* Pub. L. No. 109-3, 119 Stat. 15 (2005). Whatever the constitutional

implications of such a statute may be, that kind of law is so dissimilar to this one as to render the comparison meaningless.

Petitioner's historical comparisons fare no better. *See* Pet'r.Br.30-32. All of the state court cases petitioner identifies concern laws divorced from any broader legislative initiative. Thus, to the extent they raised the specter of "[s]pecial laws ... pushed through the legislatures by unscrupulous men to serve private ends," *id.* at 30, they are readily distinguishable from the provision at issue here. Congress did not enact section 8772 out of a bare desire "to force one party to pay other parties billions of dollars for past injuries." *Id.* at 42. Congress enacted section 8772 to ensure that Iran would be forced to satisfy the undisputedly valid judgments that the victims of its unlawful actions obtain—not just because those victims are entitled to execution of the judgments that courts award them, but because ensuring that Iran is held financially responsible for the acts of terrorism that it sponsors is a critical component of the United States' efforts to protect its citizens from the threat that Iran will continue to sponsor such acts in the future.

Accordingly, whatever concerns the Framers may have had about legislative interference in private disputes among citizens, those, too, are inapposite here. The specificity of section 8772 reflects not a congressional desire to interfere with a private dispute (or with the independence of the judiciary), but rather a congressional effort to make sensitive foreign policy judgments unique to a particular country. Iran has time and again refused to abide by international rules, and Congress is free to react by refusing to apply the same rules to Iran as it does to the rest of the international community. After all, the Framers granted Congress broad powers to address foreign relations. For those powers to be effective, Congress must be able to invoke them flexibly and sensitively to address specific threats posed by specific nations. It is thus no wonder that section 8772 is targeted at a particular country and set of assets. Foreign policy is not a place for one-size-fits-all rules; it would be absurd to require Congress to give Iran the same sovereign immunity as Ireland.

18

*   *   *

As the foregoing reveals, section 8772 is simply not what petitioner tries to make it out to be. The statute applies not to "a single pending case," Pet'r.Br.i, but to an entire class of cases. The statute does not "direct[] a particular result," whether "effectively" or otherwise. *Id.* And the statute is designed to further critical foreign policy objectives, not "to ensure that [Congress'] favored litigant prevails." *Id.* at 2. In short, the statute does not even implicate any of the constitutional concerns that petitioner identifies.

.III   **Section 8772 Does Not Violate Any Separation Of Powers Principle.**

At any rate, petitioner's conception of the separation of powers constraints that this Court's cases impose on Congress' ability to legislate is fundamentally flawed. Properly understood, the principles that this Court has articulated do not prohibit Congress from legislating with specificity, or from passing laws that are designed to affect the outcome of a pending case. They just require Congress to refrain from interfering with the judiciary's core role of deciding how *existing* law applies to a particular set of facts. Section 8772 does not interfere with that role at all.

..III.A.   **Section 8772 Does Not Run Afoul of the Separation of Powers Principles Set Forth in *Klein*.**

For all the ink that has been spilled about *United States v. Klein*, 80 U.S. (13 Wall.) 128 (1872), its core holding is straightforward: Congress may not instruct an Article III court how to apply existing law to particular facts. Courts alone wield the power to take a law as written and apply it to the facts. If Congress seeks to affect the outcome of pending cases, it must do so by using its Article I powers to amend the law, not by telling courts how to perform their Article III function of applying the law to particular facts. The statute in *Klein* violated that separation of powers principle because it purported to instruct courts how to apply the existing legal framework governing

19

reimbursement of captured property to the fact of a presidential pardon. Indeed, it purported to compel courts "to deny to pardons granted by the President the effect which this court had adjudged them to have." *Klein*, 80 U.S. at 145. This Court thus was "forbidden to give the effect to evidence which, in its own judgment, such evidence should have, and [wa]s directed to give it an effect precisely contrary." *Id.* at 147.

Accordingly, while *Klein* itself may not be a paragon of clarity, the principle it stands for is simple: Congress cannot instruct an Article III court how to apply existing law to particular facts. This Court's cases confirm that understanding. In *Robertson*, for instance, the Court was not troubled by the fact that the challenged law singled out two pending cases. Nor was the Court troubled by the fact that Congress enacted the law for the specific purpose of putting an end to the litigation that it expressly referenced. Instead, it was enough to satisfy any separation of powers concerns that Congress had not tried to "direct[] decisions in pending cases *without amending any law*"; it instead "affected the adjudication of the cases" by "effectively modifying the provisions at issue in those cases." *Robertson*, 503 U.S. at 440-41 (emphasis added).

The Court reiterated the same understanding in *Plaut v. Spendthrift Farm, Inc.*, 514 U.S. 211 (1995). As the Court explained there, "[w]hatever the precise scope of *Klein*, … later decisions have made clear that its prohibition does not take hold when Congress 'amend[s] applicable law.'" *Id.* at 218 (quoting *Robertson*, 503 U.S. at 441). And in *Miller v. French*, 530 U.S. 327 (2000), this Court rejected a *Klein* challenge to the Prison Litigation Reform Act because the statute created "a new legal standard" rather than "prescribing a rule of decision." *Id.* at 349-50. Indeed, even petitioner's own *amici* agree that "*Klein*'s central distinction" is "between directing law application and amending the underlying law," FCS.Br.9, and identify *Klein*'s core holding as the principle that "Congress may not direct the result in a pending case without amending the underlying law," *id.* at 4.[3]

Properly understood, then, the *Klein* question in this case is remarkably easy: Section 8772 does not direct courts how to apply existing law; it instead just changes the law that applies to the particular assets at issue. Congress did not instruct courts that, notwithstanding how the Uniform Commercial Code has been interpreted, attachment of the relevant assets must be found to satisfy its requirements. Nor did Congress say anything about whether the assets should be deemed attachable under the terms of the Foreign Sovereign Immunities Act, the Terrorism Risk Insurance Act of 2002, or any provision of law. Indeed, Congress could not have made clearer that it was creating a new law that would apply "*notwithstanding any other provision of law*" and was "preempting any inconsistent provision of State law." 22 U.S.C. §8772(a)(1) (emphasis added). Thus, rather than instructing the Court how to *apply* the law, Congress simply "'amend[ed] applicable law.'" *Plaut*, 514 U.S. at 218 (quoting *Robertson*, 503 U.S. at 441). That is exactly what this Court has said—repeatedly—that *Klein* in no way prohibits Congress from doing.

---

[3] In fact, the principle *Klein* stands for is arguably even narrower than that. As scholars have noted, the statute at issue in *Klein* posed a particular problem because it sought to override the Court's interpretation of a *constitutional* provision. *See, e.g.*, Martin H. Redish & Christopher R. Pudelski, *Legislative Deception, Separation of Powers, and the Democratic Process: Harnessing the Political Theory of United States v. Klein*, 100 Nw. U. L. Rev. 437, 464 (2006) ("The Court was necessarily concerned … that Congress was seeking to interfere with the judicial interpretation of constitutional provisions."); Daniel J. Meltzer, *Congress, Courts, and Constitutional Remedies*, 86 Geo. L.J. 2537, 2540 (1998) ("Congress may not compel the courts to speak a constitutional untruth."). Section 8772, of course, raises no such concern.

..III.B.   Article III Does Not Prohibit Congress From "Effectively Dictating" the Outcome of Cases.

Petitioner insists that *Klein* stands for a far more sweeping proposition—namely, that "legislatures may not dictate the outcome of pending cases." Pet'r.Br.19. That is simply not correct. It is well-settled that Congress may pass laws that apply to cases pending at the time of enactment—even when the new law is outcome-determinative. For example, in *Bruner v. United States*, this Court dismissed an action because, while the case was pending, Congress repealed the jurisdictional statute under which it had been filed. 343 U.S. 112 (1952). In *United States v. Schooner Peggy*, this Court reversed a decree condemning a French vessel because a treaty ratified while the case was pending provided for the restoration of captured property "not yet *definitively* condemned." 5 U.S. (1 Cranch) 103, 109 (1801); *see id.* at 110 ("[I]f subsequent to the judgment and before the decision of the appellate court, a law intervenes and positively changes the rule which governs, the law must be obeyed[.]"). And in *Cort v. Ash*, this Court reversed a grant of injunctive relief because Congress passed a statute while the case was pending that established an administrative procedure for adjudicating alleged violations of the statute at issue. 422 U.S. 66 (1975).

Indeed, Congress may pass laws with the express intention of dictating the outcome of a pending case. In *Ex parte McCardle*, Congress stripped this Court of jurisdiction to review denials of petitions for *habeas corpus* while McCardle's case was pending in this Court. 74 U.S. 506 (1869). McCardle's attorney argued that the jurisdiction-stripping law was aimed specifically at McCardle and thus violated separation of powers principles. *Id.* at 510.[4] This Court rejected that argument and dismissed the case for want of jurisdiction, noting that the Court was "not at liberty to inquire into the motives of the legislature." *Id.* at 514.

---

[4]   *See, e.g.*, Cong. Globe, 40th Cong., 2d Sess. 2061 (1868) (statement of Rep. James F. Wilson, R-Iowa) ("Most assuredly it was my intention to take away the jurisdiction given by the act of 1867 reaching the McCardle case[.]").

Congress also effectively dictated the outcome in *Wheeling,* a case that this Court explicitly distinguished in *Klein,* and *Robertson,* a case in which this Court explicitly distinguished *Klein.* As the Solicitor General pointed out during oral argument in *Robertson,* to prohibit Congress from legislating to impact a pending case would "essentially amount[] to a freezing theory, that the pendency of a lawsuit [has] an injunctive effect, as it were, against the Congress of the United States." Transcript of Oral Argument at 46, *Robertson v. Seattle Audubon Soc'y,* 503 U.S. 429 (1992) (No. 90-1596). It would make little sense to allow private litigants to disable Congress from exercising its Article I powers by filing a lawsuit, and still less sense to disable Congress from addressing an issue when it is most squarely presented.

Clearly, then, *Klein* does not stand for the sweeping proposition that petitioner urges. Congress *can* effectively dictate the outcome of pending cases, and it does so with regularity. *Klein* simply limits the method by which Congress may achieve that result. Under petitioner's reading, the constitutionality of a statute would turn not on the substance of the law or the degree to which it infringes on the power of other branches, but rather on the procedural posture of the cases to which it applies. That cannot be the law. Petitioner's "no dictating the outcome" principle cannot bear the weight placed upon it, either as a premise in this case or as a rule to apply to others.

Indeed, even petitioner's own *amici* recognize that *Klein* cannot plausibly be read as prohibiting Congress from passing laws designed to dictate the outcome of a pending case given the "numerous decisions holding that Congress may amend the law governing pending litigation." FCS.Br.7. In stark contrast to petitioner, petitioner's *amici* instead stress repeatedly just how "narrow" "*Klein's* core principle" really is. *Id.* at 4, 8. And rightly so, as *Klein* leaves Congress perfectly free to effectively dictate the result of pending cases by amending the applicable law; it just requires Congress to refrain from instructing an Article III court how to apply facts to existing law. In short, as subsequent cases have made clear, *Klein* is a case about *how* Congress may effectively dictate the outcomes of cases—not about *whether* it may.[5]

..III.C. **Article III Does Not Require Laws to be Generally Applicable.**

Finally, even assuming section 8772 applied to only "a single pending case" (and it does not), that, too, would pose no separation of powers problem. Indeed, petitioner's "single pending case" principle is a poor match for separation of powers doctrine, which is concerned with intrusions on other branches, not with constraints on the manner in which one branch may exercise the powers that it unquestionably possesses. If, as explained, section 8772 does not intrude on the judiciary's Article III function, then it is difficult to fathom how it could violate Article III simply because it impacts too few cases.

Although "legislatures usually act through laws of general applicability, that is by no means their only legitimate mode of action." *Plaut*, 514 U.S. at 239 n.9. In fact, Congress legislates with particularity quite often. Congress has passed laws impacting only a single bridge, *see Wheeling*, 59 U.S. at 429, only 13 forests, *Robertson*, 503 U.S. at 435-36, and only one President's papers, *Nixon v. Adm'r of Gen. Servs.*, 433 U.S. 425 (1977). And the list goes on. *See, e.g., United States v. Sioux Nation of Indians*, 448 U.S. 371, 389 (1980) (law declaring *res judicata* defense unavailable in one case); *Pope v. United States*, 323 U.S. 1, 10 (1944) (law directing court to apply a specified formula to one case); *Shawnee Tribe v. United States*, 423 F.3d

---

[5]   Petitioner's *amici* make the baffling claim that section 8772 is unconstitutional because "no new law has been made" at all. FCS.Br.17. Both Houses of Congress and the President disagree. *See* Iran Threat Reduction and Syria Human Rights Act of 2012, Pub. L. No. 112-158, 126 Stat. 1214, 1258. Without a doubt, section 8772 is a new law governing the attachment of the assets in question for execution of certain judgments against Iran. To be sure, the new law is not generally applicable, but that hardly means that it is no law at all.

1204, 1207 (10th Cir. 2005) (law giving the Secretary of the Army discretion to convey a particular piece of property); *Nat'l Coal. to Save Our Mall v. Norton*, 269 F.3d 1092, 1097 (D.C. Cir. 2001) (law exempting a planned memorial from various federal statutes).

Moreover, although Congress passed private bills with greater regularity before the expansion of the administrative state, "[p]rivate bills in Congress are still common." *Plaut*, 514 U.S. at 239 n.9. In 2012, for example, Congress passed An Act For the Relief of Sopuruchi Chukwueke, which provided that one individual "shall be deemed to have been lawfully admitted to, and remained in, the United States, and shall be eligible for adjustment of status to that of an alien lawfully admitted for permanent residence." Priv. L. No. 112-1 (2012). In 2006, Congress passed the Betty Dick Residence Protection Act, the sole purpose of which was to "require the Secretary of the Interior to permit the continued occupancy and use of [a particular residence] by Betty Dick for the remainder of her natural life." Priv. L. No. 109-1 (2006). No one has ever suggested that the specificity of these laws renders them subject to some sort of separation of powers concern.

That is not to say that Congress' power to single out particular individuals or property is unfettered. But to the extent Congress is restrained from enacting laws that do not have general applicability, it is constrained by explicit constitutional provisions, not broad structural principles. For example, the Bill of Attainder Clause bars any law "that legislatively determines guilt and inflicts punishment upon an identifiable individual without provision of the protections of a judicial trial." *Nixon*, 433 U.S. at 468. The Equal Protection Clause mandates that every legislative classification "must be reasonable, not arbitrary, and must rest upon some ground of difference having a fair and substantial relation to the object of the legislation." *F.S. Royster Guano Co. v. Virginia*, 253 U.S. 412, 415 (1920). The Takings Clause, Ex Post Facto Clause, Due Process Clause, and Privileges and Immunities Clause all likewise impact Congress' ability to single out individuals for particular benefits or burdens. It is these specific provisions—and not some vague notion of separation of powers—that prevent Congress from *improperly* singling out individuals and entities for adverse treatment.

At any rate, it is not at all clear how the scope of a statute's applicability "could in any way" impact whether it "infringe[s] upon the judicial power." *Plaut*, 514 U.S. at 238-39. Separation of powers principles are concerned with the aggrandizement of one branch at the expense of another. *See Miller*, 530 U.S. at 341 ("[T]he Constitution prohibits one branch from encroaching on the central prerogatives of another."); *Clinton v. Jones*, 520 U.S. 681, 699 (1997) ("The Framers 'built into the tripartite Federal Government ... a self-executing safeguard against the encroachment or aggrandizement of one branch at the expense of the other.'" (alteration in original)). It is not concerned with how a single branch exercises its own power. *See Touby v. United States*, 500 U.S. 160, 167-68 (1991) ("The principle of separation of powers ... does not speak to the manner in which authority is parceled out within a single Branch."). Given that section 8772 does not intrude on the judicial role, *see supra* Part III.A, surely it cannot offend Article III simply because of how few cases it impacts. Once it is clear that Congress has not intruded into the realm of one of its co-equal branches of government—and that is quite clear here—then only some *other* principle could limit how Congress can exercise its own power. By relying on the separation of powers, petitioner hangs its hat on the wrong constitutional hook.

CONCLUSION

For the foregoing reasons, this Court should affirm the judgment below.

Respectfully submitted,

ERIN E. MURPHY
Counsel of Record
MICHAEL D. LIEBERMAN
Bancroft PLLC
500 New Jersey Avenue, NW
Seventh Floor
Washington, DC 20001
(202) 234-0090
emurphy@bancroftpllc.com

Counsel for Amicus Curiae

December 23, 2015